Christmas Stories on Stage

Plays for Children

Christmas Stories on Stage

First published in 2016 by

JemBooks

Cork,

Ireland

ISBN: 978-0-9935506-0-7

All rights reserved.

No part of this book may be reproduced or utilised in any form or by any electronic, digital or mechanical means, including information storage, photocopying, filming, recording, video recording and retrieval systems, without prior permission in writing from the publisher. The only exception is by a reviewer, who may quote short excerpts in a review. The moral rights of the author have been asserted.

Text Copyright © 2016, Julie Meighan

Christmas Stories on Stage

Plays for Children

Julie Meighan

JemBooks

About the Author

Julie Meighan is a lecturer of drama in education at the Cork Institute of Technology. She has taught drama to all age groups and levels. She is the author of the Amazon bestselling books *Drama Start: Drama Activities, Plays and Monologues for Young Children (Ages 3 -8)* ISBN 978-0956896605, *Drama Start Two: Drama Activities and Plays for Children (Ages 9 -12)* ISBN 978-0-9568966-1-2 and *Stage Start: 20 Plays for Children (Ages 3-12)* ISBN 978-0956896629.

Christmas Stories on Stage

Table of Contents

Part One: Drama Games 1
  Game: Santa's Reindeer 2
  Game: What's the Time, Santa Claus? 3
  Game: Elves and Reindeer 4
  Game: Mrs. Claus's Knickers 5
  Game: If I Could Be a Christmas Toy 6
  Game: All I Want for Christmas Is... 7
  Game: Follow the Reindeer 8
  Game: Santa Claus's Glasses 9
  Game: Santa Says 10
  Game: Sleeping Reindeer 11

Part Two : Plays Based on Christmas Stories ... 12
  Rudolph: The Missing Reindeer 13
  The Elves and the Shoemaker 18
  Home for Christmas 21
  Saint Bernadette 24
  The Selfish Giant 26
  The Little Match Girl 34
  A Visit from Saint Nick 37
  The Fir Tree 39
  The Snowman 41
  The Brave Tin Soldier 44

Part One:
Drama Games

The following drama games are clearly set out and the appropriate age group and minimum number of children needed to participate are listed for each one. The benefits of playing the game are also stated, and detailed instructions are provided. All the drama games listed are based on a Christmas theme, and they can be played as part of a drama class.

Game: Santa's Reindeer

Age: 4 years+

Minimum number of participants: 7

Resources needed: Clear space and a chair for each student. If you do not have chairs, you can use sheets of paper or cushions.

Aim: This game can be used very effectively to develop listening and observation skills.

Instructions: All the children sit in a circle on a chair or a cushion. The teacher chooses three of Santa's reindeer and goes around the circle giving each child the name of a reindeer in a particular order, for example, Rudolph, Dasher, and Prancer. A child is then chosen, or volunteers, to go into the centre of the circle. His/her chair is taken away. The child in the centre is Santa Claus and he calls out the name of one of the three reindeer. If the child in the centre says Rudolph, then all the Rudolphs change place; if s/he says Dasher, all the Dashers change place and if s/he says Prancer, all of the Prancers change places. If s/he says Santa's Reindeer, then everyone changes places. The child who is left without a chair, goes into the centre for the next round.

Game: What's the Time, Santa Claus?

Age: 3 years +
Minimum number of participants: 4
Resources needed: Clear space.
Benefits: This activity is based on a popular traditional children's game that can also be used very effectively in a drama session as a warm-up game. This game also helps children with their listening and coordination skills.
Instructions: One child is chosen or volunteers to be Santa Claus and stands at one side of the clear space. His/her back is to the other children, who are standing at the opposite end of the space. The rest of the children shout out: "What's the time, Santa Claus?" Santa Claus does not turn around. He/she might reply: "Four o'clock." The children walk forward the number of steps that Santa Claus calls out (in this case, four). The children ask again: "What time is it, Santa Claus?" Santa Claus might reply: "Five o'clock." The children take five steps forward. The children continue to ask the question and to walk the appropriate number of steps forward. Eventually, when Santa Claus thinks that the children are near enough, he/she will say: "Christmas time!" Then, Santa Claus turns around and chases the children. They must try to rush back to their starting place. If Santa Claus catches one of them before they reach home, that child is Santa Claus in the next game.

Game: Elves and Reindeer

Age: 5 years+
Minimum number of participants: 2
Resources needed: Clear space.
Benefits: The children work as part of a pair but it helps them practise giving clear directions to their partners.
Instructions: This is a fun game that children enjoy. Divide the group into pairs. Child A is the Elf and child B is the reindeer. The elf must guide the reindeer around the clear space by giving them very specific directions. The elf can say for example: "Go ten steps forwards," or, "Put your hands in the air and turn around five times." The elf must make sure that their reindeer do not bump into other elves and reindeer in the group. They can switch roles after a few minutes.

Game: Mrs. Claus's Knickers

Age: 5 years +
Minimum number of participants: 3
Resources needed: Clear space.
Benefits: This helps to improve eye contact and body language. It also stimulates imagination as the children must come up with unique questions.
Instructions: The children sit in a circle. One child sits in the middle of the circle and everyone in the circle takes turns asking him/her a question, for example: "What did you have for breakfast?" The child in the middle is only allowed to answer, "Mrs Claus's Knickers," and they must not laugh or smile. If they laugh or smile, they must change places with the child whose question made them laugh.

Game: If I Could Be a Christmas Toy

Age: 3 years +
Minimum number of participants: 2
Resources needed: Clear space.

Benefits: This game stimulates creativity. It helps the children to move and to get into different roles.

Instructions: Each child in the circle takes it in turn to say for example: "Hi, my name is Anna, and if I could be any Christmas toy, I would be a football because..." The children should be encouraged to come up with unusual toys. They could also comment on and respond to the other children's choice of toy. At the end, the teacher can get the children to imagine that they are in the toy shop and then they walk around the clear space pretending to be their chosen toy.

Game: All I Want for Christmas Is...

Age: 4 years +
Minimum number of participants: 5
Resources needed: Clear space.
Benefits: This game stimulates the imagination and is very good for focussing on memory skills. It is also an excellent listening game.
Instructions: Everyone sits in a circle. The teacher starts by saying something like: "All I want for Christmas is a doll..." The child next to the teacher follows by first repeating what the teacher said and adding an item to the list: "All I want for Christmas is a doll and a PlayStation..." The next child continues by saying something like: "All I want for Christmas is a doll and a PlayStation and a guitar." The game continues, with each child repeating what the previous children have said and adding one item to the Christmas list. If a child makes a mistake, then they are out of the game. The list continues until there is only one child left in the game.

Game: Follow the Reindeer

Age: 4 years +
Minimum number of participants: 3
Resources needed: Clear space.
Benefits: This game also improves reaction and observation skills.
Instructions: All the children stand in a circle and they start walking on the spot. The teacher/volunteer is the reindeer. The reindeer makes a gesture and the children copy it, for example, waving their left hand. Then the reindeer shouts out the name of one of the children in the group and they must change or add to the action, for example, waving their left and right hands. The game can continue until everyone in the circle has had a chance to add or to change an action.

Game: Santa Claus's Glasses

Age: 4 years +
Minimum number of participants: 5
Resources needed: Clear space, glasses.
Benefits: This is an effective listening game. It can also be used to improve concentration skills.
Instructions: One child is chosen to be Santa Claus. Santa Claus puts the glasses on his head and faces a wall at one side of the clear space. The other children in the group must go to the other side of the space. They must try to creep up on Santa Claus and take his glasses. Santa Claus can turn around suddenly at any time. If he sees anyone moving that child must start again from the beginning.

Game: Santa Says

Age: 3 years +
Minimum number of participants: 3
Resources needed: Clear space.
 Benefits: This is a very good listening or warm-up game.
Instructions: The teacher is Santa and all the children in the group stand in a line. Santa then calls out an action for the children to follow. It can be any action, such as touch your nose with your middle finger, hop on one foot or clap your hands five times and turn around. Santa, however, must say, "Santa says," before the action, otherwise the children should stand still and not do anything. If Santa doesn't say "Santa says" and just states the action by itself, such as, "Stand on one leg," whoever does it is out and must sit down. The last child in the group who is left standing can then be Santa! Variations: Frosty Says, Rudolph Says, The Fairy Says, Mrs. Claus Says, The Elf Says and so on.

Game: Sleeping Reindeer

Age: 3 years+
Minimum number of participants: 3
Resources needed: Clear space.
Benefits: This helps children improve their sensory awareness.
Instructions: All the children are reindeer. They lie down on the floor with their eyes closed and stay still, as if they are sleeping. The teacher goes around the room, trying to get the reindeer to move. If they move, then they must get up and help the teacher to try to get the other reindeer to move. They are not allowed to touch the reindeer, but they may move close to them, tell jokes or make silly faces. After five minutes, tell the reindeer who are still on the floor to wake up. It is time to pull Santa's sled.

Part Two :
Plays Based on Christmas Stories

The following is a collection of plays that have been adapted from well-known Christmas stories. They can be used as performance plays, readers' theatre or just to promote reading in groups. Each play is between five and ten minutes long. The plays can be adapted to suit the various needs of the group. The cast list is very flexible and characters can be added, changed or omitted. In addition, the teacher/group leader can assume the role of the storyteller if the children are unable to read or not at the reading level required.

Props/costume/stage directions:
There is a minimal number of props needed for these plays. Costumes can be very simple. The children can wear clothes that are the same colour as their animal or their character. They can wear a mask or use some face paint. All suggestions for stage directions are included in brackets and italics.

Rudolph: The Missing Reindeer

Characters: Santa Claus, Rudolph, Elf, ten groups *(there can be as many children in each group as needed)*

Materials: A large picture of Rudolph divided into ten parts. Give one part to each one of the ten groups. A board or a flip chart is needed so that each group can stick each part of the picture on one by one. There is no limit to the number you can have in each group. Each group can either recite the rhyme or some members of the group can recite it and other members can act it out.

(Santa Claus comes out to the front of the stage and starts looking around. He looks a bit worried. He scans the sky with his telescope.)

Santa Claus: Hello, everybody. I'm looking for Rudolph. Has anyone seen him? I looked everywhere for him and I can't find him anywhere. *(He has a telescope and is scanning the sky.)*
Santa Claus: I've looked in the stable,
I've looked in the shed;
I've looked in the cupboard,
But I think he has fled.
I need help. Can you help me?
(Elf/elves enter carrying a scroll. The elf faces the audience.)
Elf: Hear ye, hear ye!
Santa Claus needs your help.
(Santa Claus goes and sits in his chair and shakes his head in despair.)
Santa Claus: Oh, dear, what am I going to do? I won't be able to deliver the presents to all the children on Christmas Eve if I can't find my reindeer.
Elf: *(Returns with all the children. One member of each group carries a piece of the puzzle behind his/her back.)*

They're here, they're here!
They've come from afar;
By boat, by plane, by train and by car.
Santa Claus: Rudolph has disappeared and I don't know what to do.
It's a puzzle to me and I need help from you. *(Points to the children.)*
(Santa Claus is in the centre of the stage and group 1 comes around him.)
Group 1: Little Miss Muffet *(rhyme can be acted out)*
Sat on her tuffet
Eating her curds and whey;
Along came a spider
And sat down beside
And frightened Miss Muffet away.
(Children say their lines to Santa Claus and they stick a piece of their puzzle on the board or flip chart that is behind Santa Claus and he can't see it.)
Santa Claus: Your rhyme is nice,
But it's what I fear,
It cannot help
Bring back my reindeer.
(The elf calls to the next group to come forward; Santa Claus is looking up to the skies.)
Group 2: Little Jack Horner *(rhyme can be acted out)*
Sat in the corner
Eating a Christmas pie.
He put in his thumb
And pulled out a plum
And said, "What a good boy am I."
(Children say their lines to Santa Claus and they stick a piece of their puzzle on the board or flip chart that is behind Santa Claus and he can't see it.)
Santa Claus: Your rhyme is nice,
But it's what I fear
It cannot help
Bring back my reindeer.

Group 3: Mary, Mary quite contrary (*rhyme can be acted out*)
How does your garden grow?
With silver bells and cockle shells
And pretty maids all in the row.
(Children say their lines to Santa Claus and they stick a piece of their puzzle on the board or flip chart that is behind Santa Claus and he can't see it.)
Santa Claus: Your rhyme is nice,
But it's what I fear
It cannot help
Bring back my reindeer.
Group 4: Little boy blue, come blow your horn. (*rhyme can be acted out*)
The sheep's in the meadow
The cow's in the corn.
Where's the little boy that
Looks after the sheep?
Under the haystack fast asleep.
(Children say their lines to Santa Claus and they stick a piece of their puzzle on the board or flip chart that is behind Santa Claus and he can't see it.)
Santa Claus: Your rhyme is nice,
But it's what I fear
It cannot help
Bring back my reindeer.
Group 5: Jack be nimble (rhyme can be acted out.)
Jack be quick
Jack jump over the candlestick.
(Children say their lines to Santa Claus and they stick a piece of their puzzle on the board or flip chart that is behind Santa Claus and he can't see it.)
Santa Claus: Your rhyme is nice,
But it's what I fear
It cannot help
Bring back my reindeer.
Group 6: Old Mother Hubbard (*rhyme can be acted out*)
Went to the cupboard

To give her poor dog a bone.
But when she got there,
Her cupboards were bare
And so, the poor dog had none.
(Children say their lines to Santa Claus and they stick a piece of their puzzle on the board or flip chart that is behind Santa Claus and he can't see it.)
Santa Claus: Your rhyme is nice,
But it's what I fear
It cannot help
Bring back my reindeer.
Group 7: Georgy Porgy, pudding 'n pie, *(rhyme can be acted out)*
Kissed the girls the girls and made them cry.
When the boys came out to play
Georgy Porgy ran away.
(Children say their lines to Santa Claus and they stick a piece of their puzzle on the board or flip chart that is behind Santa Claus and he can't see it.)
Santa Claus: Your rhyme is nice,
But it's what I fear
It cannot help
Bring back my reindeer.
Group 8: Three blind mice, see how they run, *(rhyme can be acted out)*
They all ran after the farmer's wife
Who cut off their tails with a carving knife?
Did you ever see such a thing in your life?
As three blind mice?
(Children say their lines to Santa Claus and they stick a piece of their puzzle on the board or flip chart that is behind Santa Claus and he can't see it.)
Santa Claus: Your rhyme is nice,
But it's what I fear
It cannot help
Bring back my reindeer.
Group 9: Jack Sprat *(rhyme can be acted out)*
Could eat no fat;

His wife could eat no lean.
And so, betwixt them both,
They licked the platter clean.
(Children say their lines to Santa Claus and they stick a piece of their puzzle on the board or flip chart that is behind Santa Claus and he can't see it.)
Santa Claus: Your rhyme is nice,
But it's what I fear
It cannot help
Bring back my reindeer.
Group 10: There was a little girl, *(rhyme can be acted out)*
Who had a little curl
Right in the middle of her forehead.
When she was good.
She was very, very good,
And when she was bad she was horrid.
(Children say their lines to Santa Claus and they stick a piece of their puzzle on the board or flip chart that is behind Santa Claus and he can't see it.)
Santa Claus: I'm old Santa Claus
And I'm stuck on the ground.
While that reindeer of mine
Is up playing around.
(Children say their lines to Santa Claus and they stick a piece of their puzzle on the board or flip chart that is behind Santa Claus and he can't see it.)
Everyone: Your puzzle is solved! Turn around, turn around.
(Santa Claus turns around and sees either a picture of Rudolph or one of the children can be dressed as Rudolph.)
Santa Claus: Rudolph, I'm so happy I found you. We can deliver the Christmas presents together.
Everyone: Hooray!

Christmas Stories on Stage

The Elves and the Shoemaker

Characters: Shoemaker, Shoemaker's wife, three customers, three narrators, and four elves

Narrator 1: There once lived a shoemaker who was very kind but very poor.
Narrator 2: He and his wife had nothing to eat. *(The Shoemaker and his wife are centre stage; the shoemaker is looking at some leather he has and the wife is looking around the kitchen for some food.)*
Shoemaker: I'm so hungry! I have only got this one piece of leather left. *(He holds ups the leather.)* I will leave it here and make the shoes in the morning.
Wife: Let's go to bed. *(They go to the side of the stage and go to sleep.)*
Narrator 3: The next morning, the shoemaker woke up and came downstairs.
Narrator 1: On his table, he saw the most beautiful shoes he had ever seen.
Shoemaker: *(looks admiringly at the shoes)* Am I dreaming?
Wife: *(shocked)* Who made these marvellous shoes?
(A customer walks into the shop so they stop talking, and smile and greet her.)
Customer 1: Oh, my, what beautiful shoes! I must have them. Here, keep the change. *(She gives the shoemaker money and exits the shop.)*
Shoemaker: Look, we have enough money to buy leather for two pairs of shoes and some food. *(The shoemaker and his wife hug each other and jump up and down with excitement.)*
Narrator 2: Next day, the shoemaker and his wife woke up and found two pairs of shoes. They were more beautiful than the first pair.
Wife: Oh, what beautiful shoes. Who is making them?
Shoemaker: I don't know.

Customer 2: *(enters)* I just saw those shoes in the window. Can I buy them?
Shoemaker: Certainly. *(Gives her the shoes.)*
Customer 2: Keep the change. *(Exits the shop.)*
(Customer 3 enters, very excited.)
Customer 3: I just saw the most beautiful shoes in the window. Can I buy them?
Shoemaker: Certainly. *(Gives her the second pair of shoes.)*
Customer 3: Keep the change. *(Exits the shop.)*
Shoemaker: *(looks at money)* Now I've enough money to buy four pieces of leather.
Narrator 3: Over the next few weeks the shoe shop became very popular.
Narrator 1: The shoemaker and his wife went to bed every night.
Narrator 2: And every morning there were always new shoes waiting to be sold.
Shoemaker: I can't work it out. What kind of magic is making all these beautiful shoes? I've a plan. *(He whispers to his wife. Both whisper to each other. The audience can't hear.)*
Narrator 3: So, that night, instead of going to bed like they usually did, they hid behind the table.
Narrator 1: When the clock struck midnight, four elves came tiptoeing into the room.
Elf 1: Look, he has left more leather.
Elf 2: Let's make some shoes for the kind old man and his wife.
Elf 3: They will be so happy when they see these beautiful shoes.
Elf 4: Come, it's time to leave. Be quiet, everyone. *(They tiptoe quietly and slowly and exit the stage. Shoemaker and his wife come out from behind the table.)*
Wife: They have made us rich.
Shoemaker: We must return the favour, and I've a plan. *(He whispers in his wife's ear and she nods her head.)*

Narrator 1: So, the old man and his wife worked all day to make the elves little green suits and shoes.

Narrator 2: When the clock struck midnight, the shoemaker and his wife hid behind the table again and waited. *(The Elves tiptoe in the room very quietly.)*

Elf 1: Sssshhh!

Elf 2: Look at these. *(Holds up the elves' suits and shoes.)*

Elf 3: This is the most beautiful present anyone has ever given us.

Elf 4: Let's put them on.

(They admire themselves and jump up and down with excitement.)

Narrator 3: The old man and his wife never saw the elves again.

Narrator 1: But they never went hungry again because they were so rich from selling shoes that they never had to work again.

Christmas Stories on Stage

Home for Christmas

Characters: Mum, Diane, Robert, Peter, Caroline/Mystery Person.

(Mum and the children are getting ready for Christmas. They are wrapping Christmas presents and decorating the Christmas tree. The snow is falling outside.)

Diane: *(looking out the window)* Oh Mum, do you think Caroline will get here in time for Christmas?
Peter: I shouldn't think so. The roads are bound to be icy with all that snow. *(Points to the window.)*
Diane: But she promised. She said she'd bring us presents for Christmas.
Robert: *(sighs with boredom)* I don't care if she comes. I think it is so boring being snowed in.
Diane: I wish I could go to a disco or a film or something.
Mum: *(looks at them with sympathy)* Now cheer up, Caroline will get here if she can.
Peter: *(excitedly)* Perhaps she has met with an accident. Maybe her car ran into a snow drift and she's lying out there unconscious.
Robert: *(joins in enthusiastically)* Perhaps she's been mugged and all our gifts are stolen.
Mum: *(annoyed)* Would you two stop it; you are making me nervous.
Diane: *(worried)* Oh Mum, do you think something happened to her?
Peter: Perhaps she has been kidnapped. There are a lot of kidnappers around at Christmas. Or perhaps she has been taken away in a spaceship by an alien. Honestly, anything can happen these days. We saw this programme....
Mum: Stop talking nonsense. What would you like for your tea?
Robert: I'd like chips.
Diane: A pizza.

Peter: Popcorn and chocolate sauce.
Mum: You'll have wheat flakes; they are good for you. Eat up now. *(They all sit around the table making faces as their mother gives each of them a bowl of wheat flakes.)*
All: Yuck!
Robert: It's getting very dark. Something must have happened to Caroline. *(He starts to get worried.)*
Peter: Anyway, in this film we saw an alien and he …
Diane: *(interrupts)* …pretended to be friendly.
Peter: But then he went out one night….
Diane: ….and murdered a girl coming home for Christmas.
(Loud knocking at the door.)
Diane: What's that? *(All the children huddle together.)*
Mum: Just someone at the door. Let's see who it is.
(All run towards her and hide behind her as she tries to open the door.)
Diane: I'm not answering it.
Peter: Nor me. Oh Mum, maybe it's the kidnappers with her body.
Mum: You silly children. You've got me as nearly as bad as yourselves.
(Mum opens the door and a mystery person holding a gun rushes in. She is dressed in a big coat, scarf and dark glasses and she is carrying a large sack. She throws the sack on the ground.)
Mystery Person: Get me some food. I'm hungry and cold and tired. Don't touch my sack; there is a body in there.
All: *(shocked)* A BODY?
Mystery person: I killed a man in a fight and now I'm going to bury the body in the snow. More food. I'm starved. *(Mum gives her more food.)*
Mum: Could I have a look at the body, please?
Children: Oh, no! *(They turn away, too frightened to look.)*
Mystery Person: Yes, look. *(Points to bag.)* Children, would you like to see?

Children: Oh, no! *(Very frightened.) (Mum opens the bag and starts to laugh.)*
Mum: Put that gun away, you silly girl. *(Caroline takes off coat, scarf and dark glasses.)*
Caroline: You silly children, you watch too much television.
Children: Caroline!
Diane: What is in the bag? Is it a body?
Robert: Is it a real gun? *(Picks gun up to inspect it.)*
Caroline: *(laughing)* No it's only a toy and the bag is full of your Christmas presents. I knew I'd fool you, you scaredy-cats. Mum is the only brave one in this family.
(She takes out the presents from the sack and gives each one a present.)
All: Happy Christmas, everyone.

Christmas Stories on Stage

Saint Bernadette

Characters: Anne, Marie, Jeanne, Bernadette.

(Anne is bathing her feet in a stream. She has sticks in her hands. Jeanne and Marie are collecting sticks from the ground.)

Anne: My feet are still cold. The water in the stream is freezing.
Jeanne: Yes, it is still very cold. *(She dips her foot in the water.)* I wonder what is keeping Bernadette.
Marie: She has dropped a long way behind us. *(Looks behind her.)*
Anne: I think it is time to go home. I'm not collecting any more sticks. *(Throws the sticks down.)*
Jeanne: I have had enough too. *(Throws down her sticks too.)* Besides, I'm hungry.
Marie: Here comes Bernadette at last.
Bernadette: *(comes running in and looks around)* Oh Jeanne, Marie, Anne what a lot of sticks you have gathered. I feel so ashamed but I must tell you what happened.
Anne: What happened? *(Bernadette sits and the others kneel around her.)*
Bernadette: Marie, you must promise not to say a word at home.
Marie: I promise.
Bernadette: Jeanne, Anne?
Jeanne and Anne: We promise.
Bernadette: Well, I saw a lady. A very young lady, over there. *(Points off stage.)* She had a lovely white dress and her hair was brown.
Marie: What had she on her feet?
Bernadette: Her feet were bare except for two golden roses.
Anne: Did she speak?

Bernadette: No, she just smiled and made the sign of the cross. *(She makes the sign of the cross and she looks up to heaven.)*
Jeanne: *(stands up)* I think you are lying.
Anne: So, do I. *(stands up.)*
Marie: Perhaps you had a dream.
Bernadette: *(annoyed)* I'm not going to tell you anymore. She was my lady, and I don't want to share her with anyone.
(All pick up the sticks and run down to the stream.)
Anne: Goodness, how warm the winter water has become.
Jeanne and Marie: Yes, it is lovely.
Bernadette: *(holding hands with her friends)* Let's walk home over the stream and through the mountains. It's the shortest way.

The Selfish Giant

Characters: The Selfish Giant; the Cornish Ogre; 3 parts of the wall: Sad, Lazy and Frightened; 2 Trees; Ice; Frost; Snow; Wind; Narrator/Old man; 8 Children: Anna/Billy/Cathy/Ger/Dick/Ellie/Fred/Harry; 2 grandchildren.

(Curtains are closed. The opening scene is an old man sitting with his two grandchildren grouped around him, sitting downstage left. Selfish Giant and Cornish Ogre are sitting centre stage, miming drinking tea and talking.)

Narrator/Old man: Children come over here, and I will tell you the story of a giant who lived a long time ago. He had a lovely, beautiful garden with soft, green grass. There were the most amazing flowers and twelve fabulous peach trees. However, the giant was very selfish, and he shared his garden with no one.
Old Man: He used to say...
Selfish Giant: My own garden is my own garden and no one else can use it!
Old Man: The giant had been to visit his friend, the Cornish Ogre, and stayed seven years.
(Giant and Ogre drink tea and mime having a conversation.)
Selfish Giant: I have been here for seven years, and we have run out of things to talk about.
Cornish Ogre: Yes, you have been here a long time, so maybe it is time you went back to your beautiful, empty garden.
Old Man: They said goodbye and the Selfish Giant returned home.
(Giant waves goodbye and they both leave the stage, going in different directions.)

Old Man: However, what the Selfish Giant didn't know was that his garden was being used by the local school children.

(School bell rings. Eight children run up the centre aisle and start to play with the children in the audience. They run down the side aisles and reach the steps to the stage. The curtains open and there is a wall, centre stage, with three parts to it. There is the happy part of the wall; a frightened part of the wall; and a lazy part of the wall. The lazy part is in the centre. There are also two trees on each side of the stage: centre stage left and centre stage right. The children squeeze through a hole in the wall.)

Anna: Right, I've got through! Come on, Cathy. I'll give you a hand. Mind the nettles.

Billy: Ouch! Take care, Cathy, the nettles are very bad today. Watch out.

Cathy: All right. Nearly through. *(She pushes her way in.)* That's it. Here at last. *(Sighing.)* Wonderful!

(Children chat as four more go through the hole, one-by-one.)

Dick: *(The last one is trying to get through but has difficulty.)* This hole seems to be getting smaller and smaller, unless it's my imagination.

Ellie: No, you've got that wrong, Dick. You're getting fatter. It's all that fast food you eat.

(Children all laugh and pull Dick through the hole.)

Ger: I love this place so much, and I am so happy when we are all in here playing.

(Everyone agrees by nodding their heads.)

Harry: It's been seven years since the giant was here. I know it's his garden, but he can't come back after all this time, can he?

Fred: I hope not. But just in case, we'd better make the most of it while we've got it.

(Children go off-stage. Lights focus on the three parts of the wall.)

Frightened: Wake up, Lazy. If the Selfish Giant comes back, we will be in trouble.

Lazy: The giant hasn't been here for seven years. I am tired of holding up the centre of the wall.
Happy: I love seeing all the children playing in the garden. I am so happy when they come into the garden, but Lazy, I think you should wake-up.
Lazy: I am going back to sleep. *(Starts snoring.)*
Frightened: I'm scared. I have a bad feeling.
Happy: You are always scared. Try to cheer up and be happy that the sun is shining and the children are having such a good time playing in the garden.
Tree 1: Lazy needs to wake up.
Tree 2: Why don't we ask the audience to help us?
Tree 1: That's a good idea. When we count to three, everyone must say, "Wake-up, Lazy."
Happy, Frightened and the trees: One, two, three, audience, everybody together: Wake-up, Lazy.
(Eight Children come back on the stage and the trees and the two parts of the wall freeze.)
Fred: Let's play a game of Stuck in the Mud!
Ger: No, that's boring.
Ellie: I know! Let's play Giant's Footsteps.
Billy: That's not fun.
Dick: What about Blind Man's Bluff?
All: Oh, yes!
Cathy: Here's my tie. Come on, Fred. Ready for the blindfold?
Fred: I'm not doing it.
Anna: You are a scaredy-cat.
All except Fred and Harry: Scaredy-cat; scaredy-cat.
Harry: Leave him alone, I will do it.
(Harry is blindfolded and the game begins. They run around having fun. There is the sound of footsteps.)
Tree 1: Did you hear that?
Tree 2: Hear what?
Frightened: I heard it too. Wake up, Lazy.
Lazy: I'm sleeping.
(Giant enters while the children are playing.)
Happy: Lazy, I think you need to wake up. NOW!

(All the children see the giant and they begin to squirm and then all run away.)
Giant: How on earth did those horrible children get inside my garden?
(Looks at the wall and sees Lazy only half-standing up.)
Giant: I see where the problem is. Lazy, wake up now!
(Lazy jumps up and stands at attention.)
Frightened: *(whispers)* I told you he was going to come back.
Giant: Wall, if you don't stand up properly, I am going to knock you down and build a new, stronger wall. This is my garden and NO ONE is allowed in here. I know what I'm going to do. I'm going to put up a sign.
(Giant gets a sign and puts it around Lazy's neck.)
Giant: *(Shouts at the children.)* Can you read this sign, you horrible children?
Children: Trespassers will be persecuted.
Giant: No, you ignorant children. It is TRESPASSERS will be PROSECUTED.
Lazy: What does that mean?
Happy: It means anyone will be in trouble if they come into the garden.
(Giant exits, muttering. Curtains close to change the scene.)
Narrator/Old Man: Now the children had nowhere to play.
(Curtains open. The stage has changed, as the trees are now behind the wall and they are all upstage to give the illusion that the children are outside the garden.)
Anna: Why does the giant have to be so mean?
Billy: We have nowhere to play now.
Cathy: We weren't doing him any harm.
Dick: Where will we play now?
Ellie: The road!
Fred: We could get knocked down.
Ger: We have no choice now.
(The children look forlorn and play with their heads down. They all look toward the garden.)

Harry: How happy we were there!
(The children slowly walk off the stage.)
Narrator/Old Man: Spring came over the country. There were flowers blooming, trees in blossom and birds singing. Only in the garden of the selfish giant it was still winter. The birds did not care to sing in it as there were no children. And the flowers had no heart to bloom.
Ice: Well, Frost, I think our work has been done here.
Frost: I'm looking forward to having a break.
(Ice suddenly notices the sign: "Trespassers will be prosecuted.")
Ice: Look at this.
Frost: That Selfish Giant won't share his garden.
Ice: I know. Let's stay here until the Selfish Giant learns to share his beautiful garden.
Frost: I know, I will call Wind and Snow and get them to come and help. *(Takes out a mobile phone and rings them. Wind shows up immediately.)*
Wind: What's the big emergency? I was very busy in Florida. It is hurricane season, you know.
Ice: Wait until Snow gets here and we will tell you all about it.
(A few seconds later, Snow arrives on stage.)
Snow: I'm here.
Wind: What took you so long?
Snow: I was in Lapland helping Santa. What's the big emergency?
Frost: Anyway, look at this sign. The Selfish Giant won't share his garden, so we are going to stay here until he changes his mind.
(Ice, Frost, Wind and Snow freeze. Giant enters stage left, looking sad.)
Narrator/Old Man: The giant was very sad. A year passed and he began to realise he was very selfish. One day he saw one of the children under a tree crying and he went to help him.
(Giant mimes seeing the child. Nobody else can see him.)

Giant: Please, let me help. *(He reaches under the tree and mimes lifting a child.)* I have been a very selfish giant. I will open my garden up to everyone. *(He takes down the sign and exits.)*
Ice: Frost, I think he has learned his lesson.
Frost: It's time to go. I heard there is an ogre in Cornwall who hasn't been very nice.
Ice: Wind and Snow, come on. It is time to go.
Snow: Do you have a map?
Frost: No! But I have my new Sat Nav/GPS.
Ice: Come on, let's go!
(They leave the stage. One of the children spies a hole in the wall and climbs through. He calls the others.)
Fred: I can't believe we are inside the garden again!
Dick: It's spring time.
Billy: Winter has gone.
Cathy: And there's no notice. The giant's notice is gone!
Harry: And the garden is more beautiful than ever.
(The children hear the giant's footsteps and hide behind the trees. Giant comes on stage and sees them. He waves them over. They are frightened but they move towards him slowly.)
Giant: Now I would like to join your games, if you please! *(Suddenly looking around.)* But where is your little friend?
Anna: What are you talking about, sir?
Billy: Do you mean Fred over there?
Fred: He doesn't mean me. He means Dick. *(He pushes Dick forward.)*
Dick: Did you want something *(stuttering nervously)*, Mmmmister...ssssir...Mmmister ... Ffffriendly...Giant?
Giant: I want to know where the little boy is, the one that I lifted into the branches of the tree.
Ellie: But we haven't been in the garden since you put the sign up. Well, not until today.
Fred: Then we heard your footsteps.
Anna: So, we hid by the wall. I'm sorry that we trespassed in your garden, Mr. Giant.

(All apologize, suddenly worried that the giant might become selfish again.)
Giant: Oh, no, no, no. You don't need to say sorry. I am the one who is sorry. Please think of this garden as yours now. But I wish you could tell me where the little child lives. I am very fond of him because it is through him that I realised I had been selfish with my garden. No wonder spring never came!
Ger: But this is all of us. No one else came with us.
Billy: But we will ask around in school tomorrow and see if we can find out about your little friend.
Giant: Oh, yes, please. Now I must have my rest. My old bones ache from all the playing. You carry on playing.
(Giant sits on the side of the stage and the children continue to play in slow motion.)
Narrator/Old Man: The years passed but the children were never able to find out who the giant's little friend had been. The giant grew very, very old. He could no longer play, so he sat in a huge armchair and watched the children. They all feared he would die soon.
(Giant mimes seeing the small child and calls out to him. Only Giant can see the small child. The children all stop playing immediately when they hear Giant talking. They look around but they can't see anyone.)
Giant: There he is! Come on, little friend. Where have you been? I've waited so long for you. Come and join in the fun. *(He hobbles towards the child.)* My goodness, how I've missed you! I had a feeling I might die before you came to see me again. *(Giant moves to hug the child, and then draws back in horror as he takes the child's hands and examines them.)*
Giant: Why, who has dared wound you? Tell me quickly; and I'll fetch my sword and kill him.
Small Child: *(Audience just hears the voice; they don't see small child; the voice can be done by the teacher or drama facilitator.)* No, these are the wounds of love.
Giant: *(Suddenly in awe.)* Who are you?

Small Child: Once you let me play in your garden. Today, you shall come with me to a very special garden called Paradise.

(Giant sinks slowly to the ground. The small child kneels beside the giant, makes him comfortable and comforts him. The children, aware Giant has died, sadly gather flowers and place them around him.)

The Little Match Girl

Characters: Three narrators, Little Match Girl, the Little Match Girl's father, Grandmother, Mother, Father, Boy, Girl, Stove, Christmas Tree, Shooting Star.

Narrator 1: Long, long time ago, there lived a little girl who was very poor.
Narrator 2: She had to sell matches to make enough money to buy food.
Little Match Girl's Father: Go out and sell these boxes of matches. We need the money. Don't come back until you have sold the last box.
Narrator 3: It was winter and it was very cold.
Little match girl: *(takes out matches)* I've been trying to sell matches all day but no one will buy them. I've not earned a single penny to buy food.
Narrator 1: Day turned to night.
Narrator 2: She grew colder and hungrier by the hour.
Narrator 3: She looked longingly in the windows of the houses. In one window, she saw a family laughing and singing around a large table that was filled with Christmas food.
(Family is enjoying their meal while they are laughing and having fun by the fire.)
Little Match Girl: Oh, how I would love to be inside there with that family. They look so warm and they are having fun. I can't go home because my father will be very angry that I haven't sold one box of matches. *(She shivers.)* If I light one of my matches, it will warm me up.
Narrator 1: She took out her matches and struck one.
Narrator 2: She cupped the flame to keep her warm and suddenly a stove appeared in front of her.
Stove: Come here, Little Match Girl and warm yourself by my hearth. It is very cold this Christmas.
Little Match Girl: Thank you so much, stove.

Narrator 3: Then, suddenly the flame went out and stove disappeared into the darkness of the night.
Little Match Girl: It is getting colder and colder. I dare not light another match.
Narrator 2: She did not light a match for a long time but then she whispered to herself.
Little Match Girl: Just one more match. *(Her teeth are chattering and she is shivering.)*
Narrator 3: She lit the second match and she was transported to a warm room with a welcoming fire and a table laden with good food.
Mother: Come in and sit down by dear.
Father: Warm yourself by the fire.
Girl: Have some of our food.
Boy: Then you can play with us.
Narrator 1: Just as she was about to eat the food, the match died and the magical room disappeared before her very eyes.
Little Match Girl: I'm so sad, cold and hungry. I will light just one more match.
Narrator 2: A magnificent Christmas tree appeared before her very eyes.
Christmas Tree: Come and sit under my branches.
Narrator 3: There were hundreds of candles burning on the tree.
Little match girl: Oh, what beautiful candles. *(She stretches out her hand to touch the candles.)*
Narrator 1: Suddenly the match went out and she scorched her fingers.
Little Match Girl: Ouch. I'm alone in the dark and cold again.
Shooting star: Whooosh. *(Flies across the stage.)*
Little Match Girl: There is a shooting star. My grandmother always told me that if you saw a shooting star in the sky, someone somewhere was dying. I will light one more match.
Narrator 2: Her grandmother appeared.

Grandmother: There you are. At last. I've been waiting a long time for you.

Little Match Girl: Please don't go. I know you will disappear like the stove, the family and the Christmas tree. *(She frantically lights one match after another.)* Please take me with you.

Grandmother: Come with me to heaven. There will be no hunger or cold, only joy and happiness.

Narrator 1: The next morning the family was on its way to Christmas morning mass when they saw something in the snow.

Boy: Look, there is a little girl in the snow.

Girl: She is not moving.

Boy: She is surrounded by all these burnt matches.

Mother: She has no need for matches where she is going.

Children: Where has she gone?

Father: She is gone to a place without cold, hunger or pain. Just warmth and happiness.

Christmas Stories on Stage

A Visit from Saint Nick

Characters: Elf 1, Elf 2, Elf 3, Mother, Father and Saint Nick.

(This classic Christmas poem was written by Clement Clarke Moore in 1823. It can be used as either a choral reading by assigning groups of children to read each character. Alternatively, it can be used as reader's theatre piece by assigning individual children to each character.)

Elf 1: Twas the night before Christmas, when all through the house
Not a creature was stirring, not even a mouse;
The stockings were hung by the chimney with care,
In hopes that St. Nicholas soon would be there.
Father: The children were nestled all snug in their beds
While visions of sugar-plums danced in their heads;
And mamma in her 'kerchief, and I in my cap,
Had just settled our brains for a long winter's nap.
Mother: When out on the lawn there arose such a clatter,
I sprang from my bed to see what was the matter.
Away to the window I flew like a flash,
Tore open the shutters and threw up the sash.
Father: The moon on the breast of the new-fallen snow,
Gave a lustre of midday to objects below.
When what to my wondering eyes did appear,
But a miniature sleigh and eight tiny reindeer.
Mother: With a little old driver so lively and quick,
I knew in a moment he must be St. Nick.
More rapid than eagles his coursers they came,
And he whistled, and shouted, and called them by name:
Saint Nick: "Now, Dasher! Now, Dancer! Now Prancer and Vixen!
On, Comet! On, Cupid! On, Donner and Blitzen!
To the top of the porch! To the top of the wall!
Now dash away! Dash away! Dash away all!"

Elf 2: As leaves that before the wild hurricane fly,
When they meet with an obstacle, mount to the sky,
So up to the housetop the coursers they flew
With the sleigh full of toys, and St. Nicholas too—
Father: And then, in a twinkling, I heard on the roof
The prancing and pawing of each little hoof.
As I drew in my head, and was turning around,
Down the chimney St. Nicholas came with a bound.
Elf 3: He was dressed all in fur, from his head to his foot,
And his clothes were all tarnished with ashes and soot;
A bundle of toys he had flung on his back,
And he looked like a peddler just opening his pack.
Elf 1: His eyes, how they twinkled! His dimples, how merry!
His cheeks were like roses, his nose like a cherry!
His droll little mouth was drawn up like a bow,
And the beard on his chin was as white as the snow.
Elf 2: The stump of a pipe he held tight in his teeth,
And the smoke, it encircled his head like a wreath;
He had a broad face and a little round belly
That shook when he laughed, like a bowl full of jelly.
Mother: He was chubby and plump, a right jolly old elf,
And I laughed when I saw him, in spite of myself;
A wink of his eye and a twist of his head
Soon gave me to know I had nothing to dread.
Elf 3: He spoke not a word, but went straight to his work,
And filled all the stockings; then turned with a jerk,
And laying his finger aside of his nose,
And giving a nod, up the chimney he rose.
Father: He sprang to his sleigh, to his team gave a whistle,
And away they all flew like the down of a thistle.
But I heard him exclaim, ere he drove out of sight—
All: "Happy Christmas to all, and to all a good night!"

The Fir Tree

Characters: Three narrators, Little Fir Tree, Squirrel, Sun, Hare, Two woodcutters, Wind, Swallow, two children, Woman, Man.

Narrator 1: Once upon a time there was a little Fir Tree.
Narrator 2: He was not very happy that he was so little.
Narrator 3: He wanted to grow big and tall.
Little Fir Tree: Oh, I wish I was tall like all the other trees.
Squirrel: You should be careful what you wish for.
Sun: Try not to grow up so quickly. You should enjoy the sunshine and the wind blowing freely through your branches.
Hare: Look on the bright side. I can jump over you because you are so little.
Little Fir Tree: I want to grow up and see the world.
Narrator 1: Every autumn, woodcutters would visit the forest.
Woodcutter 1: How about this little Fir Tree. Shall I cut it down?
Woodcutter 2: Don't bother. That tree is too small.
Narrator 2: The woodcutters cut down lots of trees, took off their branches and dragged them off.
Little Fir Tree: Where are they going?
Wind: Don't worry where they are going. Just enjoy being young and free.
Narrator 3: When Christmas time came, the woodcutters would take down the trees but not take off their branches.
Little Fir Tree: Where are they going?
Swallow: People take the trees and decorate them with colourful ornaments.
Little Fir Tree: Oh, how I long to be a Christmas tree.
Squirrel: No, you don't.
Hare: Stay here with us.

Narrator 1: The tree was still not happy. The next Christmas came and the little Fir Tree had grown.
Woodcutter 1: Look at this Fir Tree.
Woodcutter 2: It will make a perfect Christmas tree.
Narrator 2: They cut the tree and sold him to a man who carried him off.
Child 1: What a beautiful Christmas tree.
Child 2: Let's decorate it.
Narrator 3: After a few days, the Fir Tree was not happy.
Little Fir Tree: I have such a pain in my neck from standing up straight trying to hold up these ornaments.
(Children run around playing and shouting.)
Little Fir Tree: It is so noisy. I wish I was back in the forest with my friends: the hare, the squirrel, the swallow, the sun and the wind.
Woman: Well, Christmas is over for another year. It is time to get rid of the tree.
(She takes off the ornaments. Man enters.)
Woman: Take this tree away.
Man: I will put it in the yard.
Little Fir Tree: I'm outside at last. How I missed the fresh air.
Narrator 1: As he stretched out, his needles dropped off.
Little Fir Tree: What's happening? I'm brown and I'm withering. I wish I had enjoyed myself when I was younger. I shouldn't have wanted to grow up so fast.
Narrator 2: The next day, the man came back with an axe. He chopped up the tree.
Man: This will make great firewood and will keep the family warm this winter.
Narrator 3: The tree's life was past.

The Snowman

Characters: Three narrators, Snowman, two children, Sun, Man, Woman, Mother.

Narrator 1: It was Christmas time and it was very cold.
Narrator 2: It was so cold that it began to snow.
Child 1: It is snowing.
Child 2: How wonderful. We are going to have a white Christmas.
Narrator 3: The children ran outside and began to play.
(They make snowballs and have a snowball fight.)
Child 1: Let's make a snowman. We can borrow this broom and build around it.
(The children get a broom and mime making the snowman.)
Child 2: We can use two buttons for eyes and a carrot for his nose.
Child 1: We can borrow the end of this old garden rake for his mouth, and he can have my hat and scarf.
Child 2: At last, we made him. We better go inside; it is very cold and it is getting dark.
Narrator 3: The next morning....
Snowman: How wonderfully cold it is. I feel so strong and sturdy.
(Sun enters)
Sun: I think the world needs some warmth on this crisp, cold day.
Snowman: My goodness what is that thing glaring at me?
Sun: Snowman, I come out during the day to give light and warmth.
Narrator 1: Eventually, the sun went down and the moon rose.
Snowman: Where has the sun gone? I do hope she comes back soon.
Dog: Woof, woof! I wouldn't get too friendly with the sun. She will make you run. She makes all snowmen run away.

Snowman: I don't understand. You mean the sun will teach me to run? How wonderful!
Dog: The sun will teach you how to run down the gutter.
Snowman: Does the dog mean the sun isn't my friend?
Narrator 2: The next morning, the sun rose again. Everything glistened in snow. A man and a woman were taking a walk.
Woman: How beautiful everything looks in the snow.
Man: *(Looks at the snowman.)* What a fabulous snowman. He is so strong and sturdy.
Dog: Woof, Woof.
(They pat the dog and give him a bone. They smile at the snowman and walk off.)
Snowman: What are they?
Dog: They are humans. Humans are our masters. Really, things that have been in the world for a day know nothing.
Snowman: Then, tell me more. What are you?
Dog: I'm a dog. When I was a puppy, my owners use to play with me. They don't play with me much anymore. I sleep in the kitchen by a big stove. At this time of the year, a stove is the most beautiful thing.
Snowman: Why is the stove beautiful? Does it look like me?
Dog: Don't be silly; it looks nothing like you. It is black with fire sprouting out of its mouth. It so lovely and warm. If you look in the window over there, you can see it.
Snowman: That looks so cosy and inviting. Can I go inside next to the stove? Surely it isn't too much to ask, is it?
Dog: You are ridiculous. If you ever touched the stove, you would disappear forever.
Narrator 3: The snowman spent the day staring in the window. He longed to be next to the stove. As evening came, he saw all the family sitting by the stove. The stove gave off a warm flicker that looked so inviting.
Narrator 1: The next morning, all the windows were frosted over. The snowman was not happy.
Snowman: I can't see the stove.

(The sun came out.)
Sun: I think I will shine as bright as I can.
Narrator 2: The snowman didn't notice that the sun got hotter and hotter.
Narrator 3: He began to melt and soon there was nothing left but a broom stuck up in the ground.
Mother: At last I found my broom; the children must have used it to build the snowman.
Dog: That's the broom they use to sweep the stove. Now I understand why the snowman loved the stove so much.

The Brave Tin Soldier

Characters: Three narrators, Mother, Father, Little Boy, Brave Tin Soldier, five tin soldiers *(you can have as many tin soldiers as required),* Ballerina, two boys, Water Rat, Fish, Fisherman.

Narrator 1: Once upon a time, long, long ago....
Narrator 2: A family woke early one Christmas morning.
Little Boy: I'm so excited!
Narrator 3: The little boy tore open all the presents.
Mother: Here is your last present, son. *(She gives him the present.)*
(He opens it quickly but looks disappointed.)
Little Boy: It is an old rusty tin box. What use is it?
Father: Open the box and see what is inside it.
Narrator 1: Inside the box were six tin soldiers. *(There can be as many tin soldiers as the cast requires.)* The soldiers were made from tin. They wore bright, smart uniforms. He lined them up on the floor one by one.
(Little boy carefully moves the soldiers next to each other in a straight line.)
Little Boy: They look like brothers. I can't wait to play with them.
Narrator 2: All the soldiers were the same except for one.
Little Boy: This soldier has only one leg. *(He points at the one-legged soldier.)*
Mother: There must not have been enough tin to finish him off.
Narrator 3: The little boy played with the toy soldiers all day. At bed time, he left them in the play room.
Little Boy: Good night, soldiers. I'll see you in the morning.
Narrator 1: That night, a beautiful toy ballerina appeared. She started to dance gracefully.
Narrator 2: The one-legged tin soldier looked at her in amazement.

Ballerina: Come dance with me.
Brave Tin Soldier: I have only one leg. I can't dance.
Ballerina: Everyone can dance. Just follow me.
Narrator 3: They danced all night together.
Brave Tin Soldier: What a beautiful lady. I would love her to be my wife.
Narrator 1: The next morning, the little boy ran excitedly into the play room.
Little Boy: I can't wait to play with my toy soldiers. I will line them up by the window. (*He puts them one by one by the window.*)
Narrator 2: Suddenly, a gust of wind blew the curtains. The one-legged soldier lost his balance and was knocked down.
Brave Tin Soldier: Help me! I'm falling.
Narrator 3: He fell on his head and found himself on the street.
Brave Tin Soldier: Ouch! I can't move.
Narrator 1: Two boys were playing on the street. They were making a paper boat to sail down the nearby stream.
Narrator 2: Suddenly, one of the boys noticed the tin soldier on the ground.
Boy 1: Look at this. It is a tin soldier. (*The boy picks up the tin soldier and stands him up straight.*)
Boy 2: He has only leg.
Boy 1: I've an idea. We could put him in the boat and let them sail down the stream together.
Boy 2: Brilliant idea. Let's do it.
Narrator 3: They placed the Tin Soldier in the boat and sent him sailing down the stream.
Narrator 1: The boys ran alongside the boat shouting with excitement.
Boys: Go faster.
Narrator 1: After a while, the boys disappeared. The stream was very choppy. The boat rocked up and down.
Brave Tin Soldier: The water is very rough. I must hold on as tight as I can.

Narrator 2: Suddenly, the boat fell down a dark drain. A big, ugly water rat appeared.
Water Rat: Have you got your passport?
Brave Tin Soldier: A passport? What is a passport?
Narrator 3: The boat got caught in a whirlpool and took off. The water Rat followed very angrily.
Water Rat: *(gnashes his teeth)* Come back here at once. You haven't shown me your passport.
Narrator 1: The soldier was back in the stream. The stream turned into a waterfall and the boat tumbled into the sea.
Narrator 2: All this time, the soldier was thinking of the beautiful ballerina.
(Ballerina appears and starts dancing.)
Brave Tin Soldier: I wish I was back in the Little Boy's playroom dancing with my beautiful ballerina.
(A fish enters.)
Fish: I'm so hungry. *(He catches the Brave Tin Soldier.)* This looks tasty. *(He swallows the soldier.)*
Narrator 3: The Brave Tin Soldier was caught in the fish's stomach.
Brave Tin Soldier: I feel ill with all this to and froing.
Narrator 1: Eventually, the fish was caught by a fisherman.
Fisherman: *(reels in the fish)* Look, at this whopper. I'll make a pretty penny selling her at the market.
Narrator 2: The next day, at the market...
Mother: What a big, tasty looking fish. I'll take this one, please.
Fisherman: *(gives her fish)* Thank you, ma'am.
Narrator 3: Mother takes the fish home. She opens him and to her surprise, she finds the missing one-legged tin soldier.
Mother: I don't believe it. It is the missing Tin Soldier. I will clean him up and put him back in the shelf in the playroom.

Narrator 1: The brave tin soldier was so happy to be back in the playroom again. He was excited to see the beautiful ballerina.
Brave Tin Soldier: I'm home at last. I will ask the beautiful ballerina to marry me.
(Little Boy enters.)
Little Boy: Mother, you found the one-legged tin soldier. *(He inspects the soldier carefully.)* You don't look the same. The colours on your uniform are dull. You are no use to me anymore.
Narrator 2: He picked the soldier up and threw him in the fire. The soldier just lay in the fire with his eyes fixed on his beloved ballerina. He could see tears in her eyes.
Narrator 3: The next day, the little boy's mother was cleaning out the fire.
Mother: *(she finds something small in the ashes)* What is this?
Little Boy: *(looks at it carefully)* It is a little tin heart.

The End

Other books by the author:

Drama Start: Drama Activities, Plays and Monologues for Children (Ages 3-8)
Drama Start Two: Drama Activities for Children (Ages 9-12)
Stage Start: 20 Plays for Children
Movement Start: Over 100 Movement Activities and Stories for Children
Fairy Tales on Stage: A Collection of Plays for Children
Classics on Stage: A Collection of Plays Based on Classic Children's Stories
Aesop's Fables on Stage: A Collection of Children's Plays

www.ingramcontent.com/pod-product-compliance
Lightning Source LLC
LaVergne TN
LVHW041550060526
838200LV00037B/1218